THE COMMUNICATOR' POCKETBOOK

By Seán Mistéil   *Drawings by Phil Hailstone*

"Provides the busy executive with a very useful reminder of the importance and essentials of communication."
Susan Leigh Doyle, Training and Research Consultant, Leigh-Doyle & Associates

"Working in a multi-lingual and multi-cultural environment I am confronted every day with the difficulties inherent in achieving good communication. I found this pocketbook clear and concise - just what we are all looking for in a communication - and will certainly try to apply it in my dealings with colleagues."
Emer Daly, Principal Administrator, European Commission

"An excellent book, laden with practical advice. Everyone will learn something from it and most will learn quite a lot. Few could do better than leave this well laid out on their desk."
Michael J. Gibney, Managing Director, Nutriscan Ltd

Published in 1997 by Management Pocketbooks Ltd,
14 East Street, Alresford, Hants SO24 9EE

Printed by Alresford Press, Alresford, Hants

ISBN 1 870471 41 5

CONTENTS

COMMUNICATION:
THE CHALLENGE

1

WHAT IS THE CHALLENGE?

The challenge facing every manager, as a communicator, is the same; you cannot win if you don't try. You must try and then try again, as often as necessary.

Communication:

- Is the knitting which holds organisations together - and the thread which keeps coming apart
- Is the greatest single influence on organisational effectiveness
- Needs a lot more effort and sensitivity than is often shown
- Is based on assumptions, and debased by assumptions (no matter how hard you try!)
- Cannot be perfected

COMMUNICATION: THE CHALLENGE

HOME TRUTHS

If you really want to do something about communication in your workplace, one of the first challenges for you is to accept these **home truths**:

- Most of us are poor communicators and very poor listeners
- Few of us try very hard to get our message across to others
- When 'communicating', most of us take little advantage of the various media available to us
- We could all improve our writing skills

The truth is that the consequences of low standards of communication are far-reaching; yet most of us accept or tolerate low standards of communication in business - even when we know the cost and waste involved.

COMMUNICATION: THE CHALLENGE

CAUSES OF FAILURE

You want my attention? You may have to work hard to get it - and harder to keep it!

- The workplace, like everywhere else, contains many distractions that limit our ability to concentrate on what others say to us
- We like to blame modern lifestyles and competing pressures for such failings
- Many of us think we are good communicators; we are quicker to identify failings in others than in ourselves
- When you are communicating well, you may only be starting; improving communicating standards tends to generate even higher expectations

COMMUNICATION: THE CHALLENGE

THE RIGHT BALANCE

- Many employees will present you with conflicting demands; they want to be fully informed, and they will pay a lot of attention to what is said - but only for a short time

- As people become more aware of communication needs, dissatisfaction with current standards tends to grow

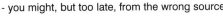

"What can I do?
Either I tell them so little that they think I am withholding information, or I tell them so much that they cannot remember it all!"

- Don't assume that you would hear if anything was wrong
  - you might, but too late, from the wrong source

THE RIGHT BALANCE

The need to communicate is too often and too easily judged by managers from their perspective alone.

Managers, more than others, depend on effective communication, in order to get the job done. All too often managers:

- Fail to see the challenge facing us all; that even when we do nothing about it 'communication' does not stop - it never stops

- See no need to consult those affected by their decisions; they depend instead on their own 'insight' into the minds and hearts of others

WHAT IS COMMUNICATION?

The working environment creates many of its own laws about what communication really is.

Several communication theories focus on the process used when a person sends an idea or message to a specific person (receiver). The steps involved in 'reaching' the target person(s) with the message include the use of signals and stimuli that trigger a response from the receiver(s).

These theories can help communicators emphasise the **exchange** of ideas and information and the **action** or reaction that arises from that exchange and contact.

Any theory relating to people can only guide us in our own experience. It does not work exactly the same way for each of us.

COMMUNICATION: THE CHALLENGE

RELATIONSHIPS

The **relationship** between the communicator and the receiver(s) (an audience or an individual recipient of a message) is what really defines communication. The audience response reveals what is understood about the communicator's 'action'.

Models of communication - 'how it works' - often tend to simplify the process in seeking to explain:

- The **need** to communicate at all
- The **skills** people possess to help them communicate
- The tools, methods or **media** available to them, and
- **How** people communicate, using their own skills and the media available to them

Communication is like a **dividend** - profits earned and shared on the basis of good planning and investment, hard work, success - and a bit of luck! Not surprisingly, that involves making assumptions.

THE ASSUMPTIONS WE MAKE

9

THE ASSUMPTIONS WE MAKE

INTRODUCTION

Every moment of the day we make working assumptions we hope will never be challenged.

Communication is full of such assumptions. Some are minor in nature and some can have a major impact on our actions and on those of others. In effect, all our relationships at work are shaped by assumptions about communication.

Some assumptions can be harmless ... yet cause outrage.

Some assumptions can be courageous ... yet give offence.

Some assumptions, in terms of their effects on the world of work, shape all relationships.

Some assumptions have little or nothing to do with work itself...

EXAMPLES

Openness and Trust

Relevance

"They don't need to hear the full story."

"What you think I need to know is not what I want to hear."

"Why are we being told all this?"

"I know what you need to know - better than you do yourself."

"Look me straight in the eye and tell me."

"What do jobs in Korea have to do with this issue?"

"We are not being told the full story."

"Forget the frills - just give me the facts."

11

EXAMPLES

LISTENING

We assume others listen.
We are often wrong.

It is not easy to listen,
even for a minute or two,
without 'translating', or working on,
the information we are receiving as it arrives.
Some of us, in typically distracting working environments,
might wait 20-30 seconds without doing some editing.
That may be 20-30 seconds longer than some of
our colleagues!

Worse than that is the tendency for those of us in the
listener role to jump ahead of the incomplete message
with possible questions or answers.

13

THE ASSUMPTIONS WE MAKE

SILENCE

Silence is a powerful, ambiguous
medium of communication.
Confusing, frustrating or wonderful,
silence **is** communication.
The silent person may be distracted,
thinking, listening, day-dreaming,
or simply pausing.

Who can tell?

SILENCE

We all need silence.
We all use it - sometimes too little, seldom too much.
We use it to listen, pause, reflect, take stock and think.

Silence allows us **not** to act like that if we so choose.
Used appropriately, silence can tell others that we are either:

- Content to listen
- Deferring a verbal response, or
- Too upset to speak

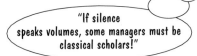

"If silence speaks volumes, some managers must be classical scholars!"

THE ASSUMPTIONS WE MAKE

LESSONS TO LEARN

1   Work on facts rather than assumptions or opinions. The only firm ground when communicating is the accuracy of the information you are using, coupled with your knowledge of your audience and their regard for you.

2   If offering opinions, make sure you do not let others confuse them with fact.

3   Work on sharing as much information as you can. If others have reason to regard you as devious, evasive or unforthcoming with basic fact, your reputation as a communicator is damaged.

4   One assumption you **can** make as a communicator: you are unlikely to please everybody.

COMMUNICATION DYNAMICS

COMMUNICATION DYNAMICS

INTRODUCTION

At its most effective, communication is highly dynamic. It has to be.

Part of that **dynamic** concerns:

- The subject or topic, be it simple or complex
- The choice and use of media in its delivery
- Its formal or informal presentation, and
- The detail of response being sought by the communicator

SIMPLICITY & COMPLEXITY

'Keep it simple', we are often told; avoid unnecessary complications in the message you want to communicate. **But bear in mind that, at the very least, we all like to put our own 'stamp' on any message we handle.**

In all our communication, we exercise influence. If and when we oversimplify the message, we may - unintentionally - convey a totally different message. At the same time, no matter how simple a **message** may be, people will complicate it.

We cannot, as communicators, forget or ignore those people who expect 'significant' or 'important' messages to be complicated!

(19)

SIMPLICITY & COMPLEXITY

When others communicate with you:

- What appears simple may, in fact, involve much more than meets the eye
- What appears complex may actually be quite simple

For your own communications:

- If it is complex, keep the message as short and clear as possible
- Look at the design, quality and relevance of the message to help you keep a 'simple' message simple - and to attract the audience attention you want; use a medium, or media, which will help you achieve those aims

"I hate to bother you"...

Even if you cannot keep things simple the same rules apply. Whatever you do, do not deceive others or yourself by exaggerating or trivializing the message. Do your best to keep the message as simple as you can.

DOES YOUR AUDIENCE UNDERSTAND?

How we communicate - face-to-face, in colour, in writing, one-to-one, in three seconds or minutes, or whatever other way we decide - can have a dynamic impact on others. But understanding is the prerequisite. How often have you heard someone exclaim in frustration, 'I just don't get it'?

Communication must be defined by **all** those who are party to it:

- If the **intent** and **content** of a message are not understood, that message is not fully **received** - and communication is lacking or incomplete
- It is not what you (the messenger) understands that matters; the receiver is the person who **confers** meaning and understanding on any message received
- The medium or media used by the communicator can aid or hinder understanding

COMMUNICATION DYNAMICS

DO YOU UNDERSTAND?

- Ask yourself, as the communicator, 'Am I clear in my own mind about what I'm trying to say to others?'
  Be honest with yourself! If you don't understand what you want others to hear or know, how can you know how to communicate effectively?

- Put as much thought into the choice of medium or media as you can afford, given the choices available to you; clearly, some media offer greater 'odds' on achieving the goal of understanding - however, there are no guarantees

Repeat the message as understood, to yourself, in your own words - and then use the best version!

EMPHASIS & EMOTION

"I want **you** here right now"

"I want you here right **now**"

"I want you **here** right now"

"**I** want you here right now"

Who we are and what emphasis we put on our spoken thoughts, together form a critical part of our communication with others.

Together, they put more than feeling into our words; they put **heart** into those words.

Whether we are 'thinking out loud' or 'speaking our minds', we are doing so through our own bodies. It is what puts **you** - nobody else - into your communication.

COMMUNICATION DYNAMICS

RESPONSE CYCLE

Without **response** or **feedback**, there is no communication. Feedback is no more or no less than:

- Body language (and contact)
- Verbal or other exchanges that indicate that people are happy or unhappy with the message sent to them
- Silence

The response cycle can start as soon as you start addressing your target audience:

- It can be slower or faster than you expect or like
- It can tell you a lot less or a lot more than you expect or like

FORMALITY & INFORMALITY

- Official, structured and written communication is usually regarded as formal

- Casual, verbal and spontaneous communication is often classified as informal

- The more formal the communication, the greater the demand for complete accuracy both in content and audience focus

- The more formal the communication, the less flexible and responsive it tends to be

- The more informal the communication, the less controlled and precise the message

- Effective communications contain both 'formal' and 'informal' dynamics, blending or fitting together to meet the specific needs and demands of each encounter

TAKING HUMOUR SERIOUSLY

- Humour breaks barriers - of culture, rank and silence
- Humour can bring levity and life into uninteresting material we seek to communicate
- Humour can make what is dull dramatic

Weighty matter becomes more attractive, easier to follow, and understand when injected with a touch of humour.

Used appropriately, humour adds meaning and depth to a message and makes communication more effective.

Bad news - more often than not - demands clear, honest delivery. All you can inject into a 'situation that is grave' is your credibility.

COMMUNICATION DYNAMICS

SYMPATHY & EMPATHY

We listen more to those we like.
We like those with whom we can identify or who identify with us.
We pay attention to those whom we believe mean what they say.

Communication is always more than a matter of words and images. It can be:

- How words sound to us
- How words come alive, especially when we hear them spoken
- How the same words can come alive every time we read them
- How images and words endure in our memory and affect us later

Communication can simply be the impression made on us by a natural and unexpected action or gesture.

Our openness will bring sensitivity, sincerity, spontaneity - even subtlety - to communication.

STAYING IN CONTROL

Remember the following 'key' to handling the dynamics involved:

- Be as prepared as you can be before you start; communication, once started, cannot easily be stopped

- Know the medium or media you are using well; without that familiarity, you can lose complete control in a moment

- Remember that most messages reach their destination faster than you plan (if they arrive at all); others will finish your sentences before you do

- There is nothing simple that cannot be made complicated, especially by others; let them do so if they wish - unaided by you!

- Communication is not always a matter of choice or timing; you won't always be as ready as you would like

THE MANAGER
AS COMMUNICATOR

THE MANAGER AS COMMUNICATOR

THE 'ESSENCE' OF YOUR JOB?

All communication at work matters - **especially when we think it matters least.**
That gives managers no choice about being 'communicators'. How can you fulfil any
of your responsibilities without communicating with others? **How can you get anything
done at work without somebody knowing about it?!**

As a manager-communicator, remember that:

- All activity results from communication

- Your **activity** communicates with others - even when you are
  not consciously addressing them

- The most effective outcomes usually follow from conscious
  efforts to communicate effectively

- Communication failures or misunderstandings are often very costly

- Direct communication - where possible - is the most effective way
  to ensure people know, understand and act, as you intend

THE MANAGER AS COMMUNICATOR

CHANNEL OR GULF?

Managers often get 'caught' in the middle (and muddle) of communication activity. Some managers see themselves as channels of communication and as go-betweens. Others see themselves as guardians of sensitive information which must be carefully sieved before it is shared. If and when communication then takes place, it may be incomplete, ineffective and irrelevant.

The key to mastering this issue is being able to handle conflict - of priority, of values, of interests, and between people within an organisation.

- **Channels** give information access, allow it to flow, give it direction and even accelerate such flow
  Do you act as a channel?
- **Gulfs** act like killjoys, swallowing information, stopping its flow or simply losing it
  Do you create such gulfs?
- **Channels and gulfs** - of all shapes and sizes - exist around you, among your colleagues at work; do you recognise them?

THE MANAGER AS COMMUNICATOR

CHANNEL OR GULF?

A SHORT QUIZ

Look at your own profile or image at work. Be honest, self-critical and realistic in answering the following questions:

- Are you perceived by others at work as an information channel?

- If someone wants to know what's happening behind the scenes, do they ask you?

- How do you address the desire of others for you to be open and to share relevant information?

- Do you balance that desire with the frequent need to maintain confidentiality?

- Do you show tact and discretion in disclosing information?

- Are you an active link in the chain of communication - or a big black hole where nothing seems to 'pass on'?

- Do you develop 'channels' of communication within the workplace?

- Do you allow 'gulfs' of misunderstanding to develop?

THE MANAGER AS COMMUNICATOR

MESSENGER OR MASSEUR?

Communicator and **messenger**
are labels that attach to the role
of manager - whether they are sought or not.

You can 'pass the message' but you cannot
'pass' on being the messenger.

No one wants the label of being a black hole
as far as communication is concerned.
If, however, you want the name of being
a trustworthy source of information, you
have to earn it.

Your action - or inaction - will often
define or label you as a messenger
or masseur of information.

"Whatever she says, she will put her own twist on it first."

"I wouldn't count on him to keep us informed."

(33)

MESSENGER OR MASSEUR?

Avoid creating expectations about communication flow, which you are not going to do your best to fulfil - or exceed.

Think about whose expectations you are seeking to meet. Are they just your own, perhaps? People entrust messages to trustworthy messengers.

Some managers 'massage' information and refashion or reshape messages. They put their own imprint on them, for personal gain, for personal satisfaction or to appeal to a specific audience. They even consciously mislead or confuse those receiving information from them.

Masseurs can become saboteurs by doctoring or changing the meaning of a communication. If you act like that, do not be surprised later if others do not trust you as a communicator.

INVOLVING OTHERS

Communication requires transmitting messages to others. It involves others. Involving others is not easy; it demands time and effort. Communication springs from needs and wants - yours, mine, other people's.

The best way to get things done (usually) is to involve others. However, this requires more than giving them tasks and telling them what to do. It means talking and listening to them.

If you exclude others from a given task you tell them that their experience, ideas or opinions are not relevant. Excluding others when they **have** something to contribute conveys its own message about the value of their contribution!

THE MANAGER AS COMMUNICATOR

INVOLVING OTHERS

As a manager-communicator, remember that:

- Employees today need to know how they are performing
- Employees should be told how the organisation is performing even when they are not seeking such information

When communicating with others, involve them by:

- Including their needs and wants
- Listening to them, and speaking to them, in their language
- Motivating them
- Putting their interests at least on an equal footing with your own
- Understanding and acknowledging their feelings

BARRIERS TO EFFECTIVENESS

WHAT IS EFFECTIVE COMMUNICATION?

We are motivated to strive for effective communication when we have important messages, instructions or requests to deliver. We achieve effectiveness when the full message, as originally prepared, is clearly understood and responded to, as the communicator intended.

Effective communication is communication that 'works'.

We do not always look for or demand such effectiveness or perfection. We must often accept much less than that, despite our best efforts and intentions.

'Perfectly' effective communication is achievable, with a lot of commitment and some luck - given how much can go wrong. Your colleagues don't really expect perfection - but they do want to see high standards and consistent effort from you as a communicator.

WHAT IS EFFECTIVE COMMUNICATION?

A LIFELINE

Effective communication is vital to all of us:

- We thirst for it
- It is a lifeline
- We appreciate it most when it is scarce
- When the supply is good, we tend to take it for granted
- It is often consumed faster than it can be supplied
- What has been 'tapped' has normally been filtered before it reaches us
- Can you imagine it not flowing?

It's a bit like water.

WHAT IS EFFECTIVE COMMUNICATION?

A PERFECT FLOW

Effective communication, like water:

- Is an increasingly scarce and expensive resource to deliver in good condition

- Is **produced and supplied** through a complex of distribution and purification treatment which is not visible, for the most part, to us as **consumers**

- Has **filter beds** which need regular maintenance

It is something of a dream now to be able to tap a mountain spring and get a perfect flow of high quality water. More often than not, as consumers - and recipients of communication - we rarely see or appreciate the work that goes into making that **flow** as effective as it is.

We are all alerted when things go wrong or the supply fails!

WHAT IS EFFECTIVE COMMUNICATION?

MEASURED BY RESULTS

Effective communication:

- Is a lot scarcer than quality water
- Is measured by results or actions
- Is aimed at informing others or changing their behaviour

- Follows, or results from, the transmission by one person of an idea, instruction or message **successfully received** by an individual or group
- Depends on action which 'fits' ideas and words
- Does not need to be very complex

Those who 'receive' your message will be quick to tell you what is or is not effective.

FINDING THE PROBLEM

When communication efforts go wrong, can you identify the source of the problem? Could it be:

- You (as either the source **or** target of the communication)?
- Others (as either messengers or recipients of messages)?
- Something fully or partly outside your/their control?

Such barriers to communication can be summarised under the following headings:

- Personal barriers
- Organisational barriers
- Process barriers

BARRIERS TO EFFECTIVENESS

1. PERSONAL

YOUR STYLE

- Each of us has a communication style, and that style becomes part of us, like a badge or pin we wear; there is really no 'neutral' style of communication

- Whatever **style** you are identified with affects your 'audience', either in a positive or negative way

- To use your communication style better, or to adapt it to the needs of different audiences, you need to understand your style and its impact

- Your style may already be your reputation, something you inherit with the job or position you hold, and it will be influenced by the culture of communication which exists in your workplace

At the very least, you are probably quite good some of the time in communicating. Others will confirm this fact for you. At least you hope so...!

BARRIERS TO EFFECTIVENESS

1. PERSONAL

PREPARATION & PRESENTATION

Thorough preparation and skilled presentation do not guarantee that commmunication will be effective. But these factors form the foundation on which effective communication is built.

Sadly, too much communication just 'happens' - by accident, haphazardly, unplanned.

A great deal of what is effective depends on you, the communicator. A certain amount depends on your audience. Sometimes it all goes according to plan!

How you plan and prepare to communicate is affected in the first instance by your motivation and style. If you care about what others think and do as a result of your thoughts and actions, why leave it **all** to chance?

BARRIERS TO EFFECTIVENESS

1. PERSONAL

PREPARATION & PRESENTATION

Ways to overcome the barriers

- When preparing a presentation to others
  - think through what you want to say
  - know your audience (what information they have and what they want to find out)
  - work on your voice to identify the tone, volume and pitch that suits the particular situation
  - keep your language as simple and appropriate as possible
  - rehearse what you want to say in order to remove gremlins

When making your presentation

- Avoid listening to yourself; let others tell you what you said

- Bear in mind that normal speech is too fast, so select a pace you feel is too slow and use pauses that you judge too long

BARRIERS TO EFFECTIVENESS

1. PERSONAL
LACK OF CLARITY & CONSISTENCY

- Clarity and consistency are cornerstones of good communication

- If you are not clear about the message you want to send, the message may not be received at all

- The clearer the message is expressed, the better its chances of being understood **as intended**, and acted upon

- A consistent approach to our communication activity can make us more confident and inspire the trust of those to whom we relate

- If your audience is not clear about the message, and satisified about your consistency, it doesn't matter what **you** think!

- Clarity and consistency on their own **'do not communication make'** - but they count for a lot!

BARRIERS TO EFFECTIVENESS

1. PERSONAL

LACK OF CREDIBILITY

You cannot communicate effectively if people don't believe or trust you.

Think for a moment: what makes a successful salesperson? One factor would be successfully communicating a specific, appealing message; credibility is another.

- We establish our own credibility initially on the basis of our subject expertise and knowledge
- We build that credibility through the experience of others to whom we relate that expertise
- Having gained the trust of others in what you have to say, you can lose it in a moment of madness (through deception, misinformation or lying - yes, lying!)

The BIG message: Never take credibility for granted!

BARRIERS TO EFFECTIVENESS

1. PERSONAL

THE TARGET OF THE MESSAGE

Every day at work, if not every hour or moment, we are all targets of communication initiated by others.

- Many 'audiences' are not really **audiences**; quite often, they are **not ready** or **not waiting** for your message
- Some audiences may be ready for you but too busy
- They may be angry, distracted or simply uninterested

As a target of communication yourself, have **you** never experienced the feelings of lack of interest or of not being ready?

Always check - when you can - whether **your** 'target' audience is ready for your message.

In your own work, you have 101 things that need your attention. Why, then, do so many managers think that others will simply be standing around waiting for the 'word'?

BARRIERS TO EFFECTIVENESS

1. PERSONAL

TIMING

Good communicators seek coincidence of timing. Their initiative should match the attention and readiness of their target audience.

As a communicator, ask yourself if you give the attention or time needed to allow your audience to absorb your message.

If you want to reduce the risk of getting your timing wrong:

- Think of yourself as a listener - as if you were listening to yourself; now think of those whom you are addressing, their needs and readiness, and your ability to listen to them

- Take time, before you start, to get the duration and timing of a message to match, as closely as you can, your listeners' situation

BARRIERS TO EFFECTIVENESS

1. PERSONAL

TIMING

Ask yourself:

- How is the communication medium you choose going to affect timing?
- How is time going to affect the medium you choose?
- Is this the only or best time to communicate?
- Are you ready to listen to your audience?
- Can you put all other concerns aside while this communication takes place?
- Can you help your audience to do the same?
- Is everybody clear about how long this exchange will take?
- Can you shorten or adapt the message if need be, without losing the effect of the message?

BARRIERS TO EFFECTIVENESS

2. ORGANISATIONAL

Most organisations are full of real and potential problems which form barriers to any attempt at effective communication.

These organisational barriers are affected by, and typically expressed in terms of:

- The organisation culture
- The physical environment
- The size of the organisation

BARRIERS TO EFFECTIVENESS

2. ORGANISATIONAL
CULTURE

Just as codes and symbols have been used by humankind for many ages, modern organisations develop their own codes and rituals of communication.

The way we think and behave, the values we espouse as members and the daily routines we observe, shape organisational life.

Inevitably, in your organisation, you will find some such features which can inhibit effective comunication.

BARRIERS TO EFFECTIVENESS

2. ORGANISATIONAL
CULTURE

Consider the range of attitudes, beliefs and behaviours in your organisation concerning:

- Consultation and participation
- Conflict
- Decision making
- Meetings
- Power and control
- Reward systems

Effective communicators - to be effective - may have to challenge current and inherited practices in these and other areas.

2. ORGANISATIONAL
PACE OF ACTIVITY

Control over timing of communication is not always a choice
open to you, regardless of your attention to planning
and preparation.

- Is everything done in such a hurry that no
  one has any time for anyone else?

- Does every message have to be
  communicated in thirty words and
  absorbed in thirty seconds?

- Are people now expected to
  process more information faster
  than even computers do?

> "Time is
> of the essence?
>
> You mean timing,
> don't you?"

BARRIERS TO EFFECTIVENESS

2. ORGANISATIONAL

SIZE & STRUCTURE

Large organisations can easily become alienating and anonymous in communication terms. Interpersonal contact faces fresh challenges in large organisations, due to factors such as hierarchy and the range and scale of activity.

People being social animals, communication is 'social'. That should mean that smaller organisations offer less daunting obstacles for the communicating manager. Perhaps - but be warned: **communicators in small organisations do not necessarily achieve greater success than their counterparts in larger organisations!**

The reality is: small units of activity do not necessarily have more time to hear or listen. However, they often expect more communication effort and success!

BARRIERS TO EFFECTIVENESS

2. ORGANISATIONAL

THE PHYSICAL ENVIRONMENT

It (almost) goes without saying that many environmental factors can act as barriers to a message being fully received.

Included among these factors are:

- Distractions, interruptions and noise
- Lack of resources or equipment to facilitate communication
- Occupational stress
- Work space, layout, comfort and heating

You cannot eliminate **all** these barriers. Identify those in your working environment. Take account of them, and adapt your message and its delivery to reduce the negative influence of the physical environment on communication.

BARRIERS TO EFFECTIVENESS

3. PROCESS

A process barrier is an obstacle to communication arising from the method of communicating used or the choice of media used to convey ideas, information or requests.

Shortcomings will often arise in the following areas:

- The channels used for communication
- Information Loading
- Response or Feedback
- Use of questions in our contacts with others

BARRIERS TO EFFECTIVENESS

3. PROCESS

CHANNELS

The channels or media used may be inappropriate, ineffective or simply wrong. They may even be in conflict with each other.

Remember that:

- Our appearance and looks influence those we target
- It is easy to forget what tone of voice can do to the spoken word
- Body language can change everything we say
- The rank or status of the speaker can add to, or take from, the message

3. PROCESS

INFORMATION LOADING

'Loading' occurs when a number of conflicting, distracting, or different messages are transmitted at one time. Some messages end up being lost or rejected.

- A basic need of any audience is to be able to cope with the information to hand before new information arrives

- Effective communicators must respect this 'need' as a right

- Effective communicators are sensitive to the ability of the target audiences to deal with a variety of messages

- Important or detailed messages are less effectively received when the 'circuit' is loaded

3. PROCESS

QUESTIONS

We frequently ask questions when we are not really looking for answers.
"**How are you?**", for example, often elicits a "**How are you?**" response, as an answer.
Ill-prepared, ill-timed and inappropriate questions create barriers in our relationships.
For example, think of the manager who asks "Any problems?" when clearly
already packed up to leave for the weekend.

Questions are too useful to confine to interview or information-seeking occasions.
We can use questions to:

- complain or criticise
- encourage
- persuade
- show our own knowledge

- deceive or disrupt
- interrupt or intimidate
- show concern or interest
- upset

BARRIERS TO EFFECTIVENESS

3. PROCESS
RESPONSE FOUL-UP

We may overlook what a 'response' is.

Messengers:

- Do not decide what a message means; the receivers of the message decide that

- Do not control reactions, feelings, or thoughts which a message may trigger

- Often discourage response by their selection of media to be used and by timing

- Sometimes do not seek any response at all

4. THE GRAPEVINE

Ever-present and ever-active:

- Grapevines produce a continuous harvest of opinions, of 'facts', of 'bad news', but most of all of 'rumour'

- The more outrageous the 'story', the sweeter it tastes

- The grapevine exists in every organisation, in the heart and mind of every individual

- It is impossible to root out - you just have to live with it

- By feeding it, you can influence it - even humour it - but you cannot control it

BARRIERS TO EFFECTIVENESS

4. THE GRAPEVINE

TIPS FOR GRAPEVINE TASTERS

- Sip slowly and sparingly

- The taste will satisfy most palates quickly

- Expect a lot of sediment - not just at the bottom of the glass

- After tasting, act with caution - your judgement will be quickly affected and you may suffer from delusions

- Try not to feed the 'habit'; you may easily become an addict!

OVERCOMING BARRIERS

QUESTIONS TO BE ANSWERED

- What are the most visible and widely acknowledged problems with communication in your workplace?
- For each identified problem, ask yourself:
  - What can I do about it?
  - What do I want to do about it?
- Who else should be involved in addressing these and similar problem(s)?

BARRIERS TO EFFECTIVENESS

OVERCOMING BARRIERS

PRACTICAL STEPS

- Identify the causes or sources of recent communication 'failures' with which you had some involvement (however small)
- Categorise these causes in terms of:
  - people contacts
  - time
  - technology
  - yourself
- Put a realistic action plan together aiming at measurable improvements in each area; your plan might include such items as:
  - planning for your meetings with others at work
  - time management skills
  - your use of e-mail, and
  - listening or presentation skills
- Set a date (say, 3 months or less) to review your plan

OVERCOMING BARRIERS

PRACTICAL STEPS

- Work hard at making each communication clear, direct, short and as simple as possible
- If it is important enough, communicate in person
- If it is not important enough for you to be there, choose a good 'messenger'
- If it is important enough, use more than one medium and some reinforcement or repetition in communicating
- If it is important enough, go over all of these steps again and again ...

MANAGING
COMMUNICATION CHANNELS

TOO MUCH CHOICE?

Managers now have more options than ever available to them in communicating with their employees, colleagues and customers. Many opt to use electronic mail, in particular, in the array of new 'solutions' offered by information technology. For some the choice is bewildering; for others it is attractive and welcome.

Is this really a problem?

More choice is not in itself making the manager's task as communicator easier. Managers must relate the medium or media, speed, setting, tone and depth of content to specific audiences.

That much can be done - so why is there still a problem?

Very simply, because we make mistakes! Our speech, our writing, our body language, the choice of media we use often leave a lot to be desired. The everyday tools of the trade for communicators remain largely the same - despite the welcome arrival of e-mail and other innovations.

THE SPOKEN WORD

Speech, the first and apparently simplest channel for communicators, brings its own problems.

The spoken word can be:

- Irresistible to me but irritating to you
- Easily uttered but less easily forgiven or forgotten
- Easily muttered and frittered away
- Sadly unheard when it might do good
- Thankfully unheard on occasions when it might damage
- Simple yet subtle in meaning
- Problematical and profound
- Frequently abused and confused
- Heartening and hurtful, infuriating and inspiring
- Often more inconcise and imprecise than the written word
- Often sought, less often 'sound'
- Wilful, wily, wise and wonderful

THE SPOKEN WORD

Loose tongues lose no time

- The urge to speak or respond to others is so natural that it often contains more saliva than sense
- Restrain yourself; get tongue-tied more often!
- Avoid the urge to feed the grapevine by repeating the last piece of gossip you just heard; wait and see how long it takes for someone else to tell you (again)

Talking less can achieve more

- Practise communicating with fewer words
- Practise communicating **without** words
- Fewer words can increase the net value of what is said; less said allows others more time to express themselves - and allows you to listen more!

Vanity and verbosity are kindred spirits

- Try speaking in monosyllables more often; it is not easy!
- Take a speech or set of notes of your own - ask someone else to re-write the contents in simple, plain words; even **you** will understand more!

THE WRITTEN WORD

"If it's important enough, you'll write it down."

In today's rapidly changing workplace, writing still remains as important an element as ever in organisation communication. Witness the growing volume and variety of written information, some of which is now subject to data protection regulation.

Demands for storing and accessing data continue to increase. So also do the responsibilities imposed on managers in the handling of data.

These factors should make managers more wary of written communication in its various forms and mindful of its accuracy and relevance.

THE WRITTEN WORD

"If it's written, you take it seriously."

"If you take it seriously, you write it well."

The challenge with writing is clear and simple: to get a message across as briefly, clearly and simply as you can.

Effective communicators are keen to find the best use of the written word. They have to be aware of the competition for attention from many other types of written material. They must also acknowledge the higher standards expected by their readers.

Golden Rule in Writing:

Do not inflict on others what you will not accept yourself. For example, do you accept 'sloppy' writing? If you cringe when you come across misspellings or omissions in the work of others, why not ensure that you do not repeat such mistakes?

TIPS FOR SUCCESS

Effective communicators:

- Organise themselves; they are as brief and clear as possible
- Know what they want to say, about what, to whom, and why - in as few words as possible!
- Keep the reader in mind at all times, knowing that readers differ in language skills and their needs and expectations as well as their openness and readiness for communication
- Know they do not control interpretation of what they write - and allow for that fact
- Balance impact with perfection, knowing that many readers have limited ability to concentrate and are easily distracted
- Generate response and reaction in as many ways as they can

VISUAL COMMUNICATION

Many aspects of visual communication (such as attitudes to dress and reaction to images) can be influenced but cannot be controlled. In other words, be wary of others' perception of what they see!

Everything counts in visual communication - from appearance, gesture and movement, to numbers, pictures and symbols. Sometimes, it may be the absence of some visual element, such as colour, which makes an impact on your audience.

As a communicator, you will all too often have to compete with the expectations and standards set by mass media, such as television.
When you do compete, don't expect to win!

VISUAL COMMUNICATION

In the workplace, visual communication 'packages' your message. For example, charts or illustrations, alongside numerical data, can help to highlight key words or text passages.

'You must have colour' to ensure effective communication, you will often be told. Perhaps. Colour can:

- Draw and help retain attention
- Be simpler, less ambiguous
- 'Reach' vast audiences more quickly than plain black and white words

For the messenger, colour carries basic advantages. Coloured diagrams, pictures and symbols communicate powerful messages. Coloured codes can be very effective (as with 'yellow for danger' in British Standard Labelling) in 'selling' messages.

VISUAL COMMUNICATION

Colour illustrates many of the limits of visual communication.

Over-reliance and overuse carry risks of:

1   Dimming attention and numbing the senses - just as boring speeches can

2   Distracting attention through extravagance - where the 'frame' outshines the 'picture'

3   Misinterpretation: for example, black is not a universal symbol for mourning

Your challenge with 'visuals' is:

●   To make the best use of those visuals available to you, and

●   To maintain as much control as you desire of the exchange with your audience

NON-VERBAL COMMUNICATION

For all the advances with written and spoken language and with visuals, there are many codes and signals, other than language, that we all use.

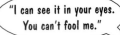

"I can see it in your eyes. You can't fool me."

Non-verbal tools remain powerful, often dominant, influences on our patterns of communication. From facial expression to tone of voice, from body movement to use of space, we continually communicate with one another non-verbally.

Some observers suggest that non-verbal communication (such as body language) is over-emphasised. However, it remains a real minefield of uncertainty. If disregarded, non-verbal communication can totally negate the purpose of communication.

(77)

MANAGING COMMUNICATION CHANNELS

NON-VERBAL COMMUNICATION

The key areas for your attention are:

Awareness   The amount of eye contact we make in conversation with others; how much, and how consistently, we express physically our feelings of enthusiasm, concern or distress

Change   The way some of these codes and signals have changed and continue to change (for example, dress code)

Contrast   How these patterns of communication can work differently with individuals and with groups, even within the same environment; what 'works' for you may not for me

Sensitivity   Acknowledgement of the need for personal space and for established boundaries and behavioural norms; the meaning others attach to physical contact

OFFICE TECHNOLOGY AND MULTIMEDIA

Communication and communications in most organisations are being reshaped by the rapidly growing use of business communication tools. Most of us now use, need to know about, or are investing in tools such as data and fax telephone lines, electronic mail and interactive video.

Some companies also have computer learning centres, network computer links and videoconferencing.

These tools rely on individuals to use them effectively for all of us to benefit.

Clearly, they can compensate for the absence of face-to-face communication - but not replace it. They can make life simpler, eliminate physical boundaries and keep us in touch.

However, they remain tools in our hands as communicators.

OFFICE TECHNOLOGY AND MULTIMEDIA

Are the recent advances in information technology making communication at work easier and better?

As speedy communication tools, their full potential has yet to be identified. The spread of much of the newer technology into the homes of millions of citizens is expected to lead to a revolution in communication access. The 'information superhighway' potentially means that people can work anywhere and communicate about anything to anyone with whom they are 'connected'.

As a manager, I'm not sure I like that notion. Should I?

Remember the underlying purpose; leaving all the hype aside, these tools can help individuals and organisations communicate more effectively. In particular, they can help you communicate speedily.

SPEED

For some communicators, speeding up 'delivery' is critical. For them, e-mail and the internet are a major boost. For some - including managers on e-mail! - slowing down the pace of delivery is important. They face information 'overload' as they struggle to absorb or digest, and then act upon, relevant items which have been 'communicated' to them.

As a communicator, remember that:

- The speed of the message is not the speed of delivery alone; the risk is that receipt of a message is not distinguished from response or action

- Whatever action you take, using the channels available to you, you cannot gain complete control over the full process

- Digital access, over a PC or modem link, or screen to screen visual connections, can be speedy and productive, yet detached

MANAGING COMMUNICATION CHANNELS

SPEED

Are these tools helping managers and organisations save time and money?

Do not forget, with the communication tools at your disposal, what the purpose of your communication is.

Remember that:

- The spoken word reaches our ears at an average of less than one quarter the speed at which we are thinking
- You should 'set' the speed of 'delivery' of your communication according to the needs and expectations of your intended listener
- The speed and range of the newer tools cannot replace human contact
- The choice and number of media in use can help speed or slow the 'delivery', and simplify or complicate the message

YOU AS COMMUNICATOR

YOU AS COMMUNICATOR

KNOW YOURSELF

Who can tell you when you communicate effectively? Yourself? Others?

As a communicator you often are, and will be, entirely on your own. Never mind the 'props' or technology, communication of your thoughts is **your** responsibility. It is for you to communicate **yourself, your intentions, your expectations** and **your needs.**

Most of all, you communicate your own confidence. If you are confident and relaxed, your ability to communicate effectively will grow and grow.
You probably think you know your own style well and you might not want to discover anything 'new' about yourself as a communicator.

What you will discover about yourself from others is often a lot more valuable than what you **think** you 'know' about yourself. Despite what you may think, your style is no secret. Others can tell you what type of communicator you are. Two communicator types - **conscious and good news communicators** - are described here.

CONSCIOUS COMMUNICATORS

- Know about, and take account of, how any communication can go 'wrong'
- Carefully think through what they seek to communicate
- Strive to overcome any possible barriers to effective dialogue with others
- Actively seek and use feedback in their interactions with others
- Deeply appreciate the need to listen

COULD THIS BE YOU?!
A CONSCIOUS COMMUNICATOR?!

Be patient! The picture becomes clearer as you read on.

CONSCIOUS COMMUNICATORS

- Recognise and adapt to different contexts of communication - with individuals and with groups
  - in person, or
  - using indirect channels
- Work with the aim of getting the correct message across
- Continually work to improve their own skills of communication
- Are sensitive to the timing of communication
- Are a fairly rare species

IS IT STILL YOU BEING DESCRIBED HERE?

To be effective at communicating you need to be a conscious communicator - and there are many people who can prove how hard that is.

YOU AS COMMUNICATOR

GOOD NEWS COMMUNICATORS

- Are most enthusiastic about, and like to be identified with, any message that has a 'feel good' factor
- Prefer to delegate communicating bad news to others
- Tend not to listen; as a result, they are poor messengers of the 'full story', mainly because they don't hear it in the first place!
- Like making the **right** headlines
- Like being in control of the message
- Are acutely sensitive to 'sell by' dates - they like to handle good news when it is hot

Do you recognise yourself here?
The tall one! Well done!
At least you are now beyond the 'denial' stage.

COMMUNICATING WITH INDIVIDUALS

Don't underestimate the importance of the **utterly unimportant.**

Those utterly unimportant words can mean a lot.
Greetings exchanged between colleagues, between
managers and workforce in casual encounters, often
convey much more than we imagine. These greetings
can contain much hidden meaning.

Very often, the **words** are relatively meaningless but the
greeting is acknowledgement and recognition - and
that's what matters to the person who looks for or
values such individual attention.

This may involve ritual - an element of communication
which we ignore or devalue at our peril.

COMMUNICATING WITH INDIVIDUALS

All of us like and value individual attention some of the time. We need such attention more than we will often admit.
One-to-one attention is communicating.

Involving others in our conversation is the most basic recognition of them.
Recognition is communicating.

Sharing our ideas, opinions, and thoughts with other individuals can bond relationships.
Bonding is communicating.

Persuading another person to perform a specified activity on our behalf can be difficult.
Influencing is communicating.

YOU AS COMMUNICATOR

COMMUNICATING WITH GROUPS & TEAMS

Within groups and teams, communication meets a number of fundamental needs.

In a number of both formal and informal ways, communication:

- Assists the process of gelling groups or teams together
- Helps clarify the purpose and aims of the group or team
- Is the means by which expectations and standards are established
- Strengthens group or team identity and sense of belonging
- Strengthens individual identity and acceptance

Surely the manager cannot be held responsible for all that happens in groups and teams?

As a manager, even when you are not a member of such groups or teams within your area of responsibility, you carry responsibility for ensuring that your communication efforts address these basic needs.

COMMUNICATING WITH GROUPS & TEAMS

Communication within groups and teams underpins the network of relationships that gives groups and teams their cohesion.

Can you say that again?

If you don't encourage and support the groups and teams you set up or inherit, you hamper communication. If you don't communicate with them and provide clear direction, you hamper their work.

The reason groups and teams exist is to complete a specific task or achieve a particular goal for the organisation. Communication draws them together, sustains them and shapes their existence. The success of many projects stems from the resources provided by those who establish projects.

As a manager, you can expect credit and recognition for your success in resourcing and supporting projects and teams which liaise with or report to you.

CHECKLISTS

CHECKLISTS

INTRODUCTION

The purpose of these checklists is threefold:

i) To help you reflect on yourself as a communicator

ii) To guide your thinking on practical ways of improving communication skills

iii) To help you work on improving standards of communication

CHECKLISTS

YOU AS COMMUNICATOR (1)

1 How much time (hours per week) do you spend on communication at work?

2 How much of that time is spent a) talking and b) listening?

3 List at least 3 media you regularly use as a communicator.

4 Do you tend to rely on one medium of communication more than others?

5 Do you give much thought to the need to communicate?

6 Are you generally prepared when you seek to communicate?

7 Do you normally plan your message or what you are going to say?

8 Do you rehearse your message?

9 Do you seek feedback on your ability as a communicator?

10 Do you welcome feedback that is:
   i) unsolicited, or
   ii) negative?

95

YOU AS COMMUNICATOR (2)

1. Do you satisfy yourself that you have done enough work in identifying your target audience?

2. Do you know the language your audience expects and understands?

3. Do you check out the emotions of your target audience and their readiness to listen?

4. Do you plan to deal with the emotions of your audience - especially if your news is upsetting?

5. Are you prepared to repeat your message if the first effort is a disastrous failure?

6. Are you ready to cut short a communication exercise if need be?

7. If your message is not fully transmitted, do you:
   i) know yourself, or
   ii) depend on others to tell you?

8. Do you seek to exercise any control over the environment within which you are seeking to communicate?

CHECKLISTS

YOU AS COMMUNICATOR (3)

1 Do you believe that everyone has a sense of humour waiting to be tapped?

2 Do you use humour in communication?
   a) occasionally
   b) consciously and selectively
   c) frequently
   d) rarely if ever

3 Do you believe that the best communicators are spontaneous?

4 When listening to others do you:
   a) concentrate on the detail of what is being said, or
   b) keep your attention on the general or overall argument or message?

5 To which of the following do you listen most?
   a) those who report directly to you
   b) colleagues of equal rank
   c) people more senior than yourself
   d) your family or friends
   e) other contacts outside the organisation

(97)

YOU AS COMMUNICATOR (4)

1. Do you avoid 'bad news' or hesitate to pass it on?

2. Do you pass on to others the task of communicating 'bad news'?

3. Do you 'manage' by working around problems or by fudging issues which you should discuss frankly and openly?

4. Are you an active participant within groups and teams?

5. Are you regarded as a good listener by others?

6. Do you regard yourself as a good listener?

7. Are you regarded as a confident public speaker by others?

8. Is this your own view of yourself?

9. Is your communication style at work similar to your communication style outside work?

10. Are you aware of your non-verbal habits and mannerisms as a communicator?

GROUPS & TEAMS (1)

1 Is there normally a huge imbalance in verbal contribution when you meet as a group or team?

2 Are there members who say little or nothing?

3 Is this low verbal contribution:
   a) by choice?
   b) because they get little chance to say anything?
   c) because they need to be encouraged?
   d) for other reasons?

4 Is there too much talk and not enough listening?

5 Is there too much talk and not enough action or conclusion?

6 Is informal communication by group or team members highly valued or encouraged?

7 Is communication within groups and teams in your organisation discussed openly?

GROUPS & TEAMS (2)

1   Is active and balanced participation - in word and deed - encouraged by you or other group and team members?

2   Is communication skill a priority when selecting project groups or teams?

3   When group or team co-ordinators are being identified, is communication ability an essential factor?

4   Do groups and teams, when they meet, always have rooms, facilities and equipment available to them to support the success of their meetings?

5   How do you communicate with groups and teams within your area of responsibility?
    a)   meeting the full group/team face to face
    b)   meeting the co-ordinator or leader
    c)   through written communication normally
    d)   when reports and presentations are made

WITHIN THE ORGANISATION (1)

1   What communication media are used in your organisation?

2   Are you happy you are using the right media or right combination of media in communicating with each other?

3   How many employees will rate formal channels of communication more highly than informal channels?

4   Do you know which media your audience(s) like(s) and why?

5   Is communication typically pursued in a hurry?

6   Is time important at all in communicating within your organisation?

7   Have you really got time to hear what the organisation is saying to you?

CHECKLISTS

WITHIN THE ORGANISATION (2)

1 Is your organisation cautious and slow in disclosing information about its performance?

2 How does your organisation respond to criticism?
   i)   directly, fully and quickly through senior management
   ii)   indirectly and briefly through PR or legal spokespersons
   iii) by trying to ignore it
   iv)   slowly or by waiting as long as possible

3 How does your organisation handle uncertainty?

4 Does it wait for trouble to 'die down'?

5 Does it act as if it would like to 'wish away' problems?

6 Are you satisfied with the communication image of your organisation? If not, can **you** do anything about it?

About the Author

Seán Mistéil, BSocSc NDPM MSc (Mgmt) MIITD is an independent trainer and consultant. He has over 20 years' experience in the Irish public service, mainly in the development and training field. He was closely involved in major organisation change programmes in the Irish Telecommunications Service and the Irish Peat Board. He previously worked with the Irish Civil Service Training Centre and with a number of Government departments.

In recent years he has contributed to a range of third level courses and degree programmes, specialising in communication skills, personal development, small business development and personnel management.

The author can be contacted at:
14 Sydney Avenue, Blackrock, County Dublin.

Other titles in the Pocketbook series include: **The Business Presenter's Pocketbook**
and **The Business Writing Pocketbook** (illustrated).

The Management Pocketbook Series

ORDER FORM

Your details

Name _____

Position _____

Company _____

Address _____

_____

_____

_____

Telephone _____

Facsimile _____

VAT No. (EC companies) _____

Your Order Ref _____

Please send me:

	No. copies
The Communicator's Pocketbook	
The _____ Pocketbook	
The _____ Pocketbook	
The _____ Pocketbook	
The _____ Pocketbook	
The _____ Pocketbook	
The _____ Pocketbook	

MANAGEMENT POCKETBOOKS
14 EAST STREET ALRESFORD
HAMPSHIRE SO24 9EE
Tel: (01962) 735573
Fax: (01962) 733637

MANAGEMENT POCKETBOOKS